BOYHOOD RISING
Seeing Through The Eyes of a Child

by TOM TYPINSKI

TOM TYPINSKI

DEDICATION

To Thomas John II, Zachary Neil, and Spencer Blake;
who continue to help me see with new eyes.

CONTENTS

TOM TYPINSKI

BREATHING BOY

I could watch you breathe
for hours on end
perched upon my knees.

Your birdlike squeaks
the moans you make
deep in sleep

Your eyelids blink
dreaming of darkness
of futures and past

You need not speak
I am content
to watch you breathe.

BECAUSE

Boys have grass stains, Ma
All the boys got 'em.
We dive at grasshoppers,
and linedrives
and interceptions.

We trip alot
from this body we got
that changes each day we wake up.

We're one with the earth, Ma
straight up and running
for passes
for baskets
for butterflies or
the fun of it.

Boys have grass stains, Ma
like Arthur had armor
and Patton had jetfighters
and boys have mothers like you.

THE MUTUAL ADMIRATION CLUB 7-87

Face up young son
How you beam
Your life seems so dreamy

I envy your position
of always looking up
to stars, to new starts,
to your world, to us.

You need not understand
you simply are
without reason

Your questions but a potpourri
of wonderment in the simpleness
that is your life at One.

And we
merely just companion travelers
on the road to reverie.

BOYS SONNET

Don't stand in the shadows of anyone
Stand in the light of the sun and you'll grow
Be confident, know which mistakes to shun
What lessons to learn from, which plans to sow
Carry the weight of all the knowledge you
Can muster in your mind, hitch up you soul
To the meaningful things like morning's dew
Leaving behind the material coal
Be the hero you hold as your ideal
Set your own standards for your visions
Invent your destiny, stay simple as a wheel
Guide your goals on tracks of decision
Stay away from the shadows of doubt
Never be in awe, but aware of your clout.

SON FLOWERS

In this dream you wear
this cute, ruffled sun dress
with flowers
all around you and on you
against blue backgrounds
color-dotted-paintball-pixilations
for the bouquet you shape
holding life controlled
in touch, tenderness and breath

as you sing a sigh of "thank you"
holding sunflowers to your breast
daintily punctuated by
10 perfect pink toes
each one a shot, a dose,
a romance aphrodisiac
a remanence of episodes
in other fields
down other roads

Feeling special to be witness
to you, to your scent
I drink in, as if eyeballs are straws
and you a fountain
your body, your skin

Thanking God for His presents
and you for this time in heaven
watching you tend your garden
in which you grow only
Son Flowers.
I watch as you nurture another.

TOMORROW CHILDREN

On sunshine's rays
or moonglow's shadows
two angels dance with glee

One blonde and fair   One brown eyed, dark
blue eyed and square   his beauty stark
       he looks alot like me   on his mother's side is he

Two angels play
exchanging blows
proving youth's a treat.

HEARTBEAT

THUMP   thump   THUMP   thump
THUMP   thump   THUMP...
...your tummy talks to me.

Curled inside
for a nine month ride
lies Baby, asleep, dreaming.

<u>IN TIME TO BE LATE</u>

Mom's and Dad's sideline their evenings with cheers and snacks and trying to learn all the kid's names. It always happens that for weeks on end they stand in heat and rain, loyal fans, watching their child's early exams on integrity, sportsmanship, discipline, ability; without seeing once an outstanding slap-them-on-the-fanny play. Then, the day you work late, they deliver, "two outs, down by three, bottom of the seventh, he homers to save the game…"

Those moments weren't really made for Kodak, they were given, created, for you. Life's lessons lived within bounds, mitts and bases, stations; like the Catholic with his cross to bear, "should I steal second? Am I safe? Do I dare?"

Each time you go to bat it's a confession, a marriage of wills. You approach with extreme unction, dying to do good. Sometimes a sacrifice fly or bunt redeems, for that last out, last inning, with two men on. The field seems symbolic and symbiotic with avenues like work, family, creativity, desperation, self-esteem. Each day a new game on a new field with new foes and different sets of rules.

Let those precious moments ring. Let every detail and nuance of touch, taste and feel capture that second where reckoning peals in to set you like a monument where earth and air mingle, frozen and timeless; able to describe it feelingly real.

It's only a moment and though I try to see each at bat I realize too, the pressure of "hitting one for Dad" lifts, lifting you to those higher moments.

Tell me about it. Make me see that you were happy to experience that moment, express that joy, live in that memory; and retell it with exuberant feeling. It is yours. I've had mine. I'm always in time to be late.

DREAMS ARE FREE

Lay down
go to sleep
and call God in the morning
with a thank you for the
things you've see
the places you'd been
in dreams

The more you thank Him
the more He'll give
Dreams are free

Lay down
slumber
in hypnagogic trance
a dance of characters
only you could create

Each you
Every facet
mirrored glass
magnetic
pulling the threads
in uncommon scenes

Lay down
Dream
Receive them
they're free.

AHOY BOYS

Bobbing brown and blonde heads
in a boat
on a lake
in the summer
one weekend
removed from bedrooms
to the vast blue and green
of sky and sea
fisher boys
fisher men

Bobbing brown and blonde heads in a boat
on a lake
taking turns
hooking worms
"cast in…
now yours…
Dad, it fell off again…"
We buy lunch for the fish.

Like childhood,
full of sunshined adventures and bliss,
summer shouldn't end.

DANDELION AT 5

blonde spikes glisten
as you rush at the wind

legs pumping pistons
as bike wheels spin

back tanned, nose freckled,
blue eyes like the sky

I stand, truly tickled
by my little guy.

THE LION ROARS

The demand from the 3 year old
bold little lion came
"take off my training wheels,"
so of course, I obeyed.

Tickled by such bravado
we rolled to the sidewalk
and he sprang away
like a dart from a gun

set me running and laughing
full of glee in seeing my son
ride unsupported, without wobble,
chanting, "let go of me,"
unaware I'd lagged by 20 paces.

No crashes, no scraped knees
just a wide smile for me
full of pride and accomplishment
self confidence in stride
as he ran to tell his mother
of his latest, greatest deed.

NOT

May love always be there
When everything else is not
May love guide you, and remind you
That you are not,
Alone.

THE TEST YEARS

I kiss your temple
as your face snuggles the pillow
and though it is dark, I sense
your smile upon my arrival.

Your warmth is irresistible,
I'm drawn to your heat.
The hairs at your nape
tickle as I breathe.

Even your scent
Your fragrance…so clean
I reach fast to touch you,
To hold you, to feel.

Your pulse jumps to fingers -
to heart, to me.
Our shield of Oneness grows
while you dream.
Just let me rest my head on your skin.
Kiss!
I love you.

SUN DAY

Clouds
sun day
no way
stay inside and watch women
and men play doctors,
and other real people.
with real people out there
working hard to be t.v. men and women.

Dreaming,
seeing every thing always
through other's imaginations
that will never be.

Cats lie and pant in shade
hot as the sun,
pool water warm
hardly refreshing
catching children
at the end of their run.

To some, summer's dreadful,
to others, lazy fun.
To one, images of hot days
when Youth still meant Young.

HEART STRINGS

Spencer's talent show

where he shines "like a guitar"

in the light amid drumbeats

of adrenaline and heartpumps

kids squirming, parents pawing

proud of their offspring

doing things they wish

they'd done more of

or identical to

in their youth.

ONLY YOU

I am so thankful I taught my sons
the love of music
the music in speech
the rhythm of writing
the words we latch onto
to define our lives

I"m so glad they understand
where I'm coming from
whether they agree, or not;
save it for later
save the sorrow
save regrets
save them to forgotten
then resurrect the blessings.

<u>YOU MAKE MY DAY</u>

Along the shores of the
Gulf of Mexico
Lie stones as blue
as bright as your eyes
holding experiences of lives
past tense and future present.

Your overwhelming sense of the regular
sets my mind in a whirl.
The soul which you hold
has been around for ages

You are a sage
you know more than I ever will.
I envy your brilliance,
I envy your shine,
I'm a gem of undeclared
value while you're worth
a million lifetimes.

Though I taught you
you've exceeded me,
in you I want to live.

Though I know you'll never
be me, I surely hope you
see me, for you're 2nd
and you'll pick up where I left off.

I only hope I've been the good example for you to top.
I'm pop, and also circumstance,
I'm a man of many chances.

Though I've
deviated from the norm,
I've loved only mom,
I am a man who attracts
from deference,
I try hard to be loved
but it's never enough for me.

MUTINY OF YOUTH

My view looks out over
the sea and the pool
a schooner drifts off
to watch a sun set
a crew of partiers
modern day pirates
carouse, shout and spew
on their dusk cruise
to where the sun drops,
extinguished by the still
sea of evening, where light
becomes new, awakens the pirates
from stuporous slumber
to begin their mutiny on life,
day two.

But I drift to you
who now sets our sons down
to rest, to become new in the light,
in the light life has given them.
They are full like the schooner and
their journey is joyous and boisterous and new,
dangerous only in respect to
what lays beyond where the sun drops from view.
They are the crew who steers us
in their mutiny of childhood
and parents and rules,
stretched to limits and laughing every minute
at the absurdity of ever
being swallowed by the sea,
of dropping off, or out of
existence because to them
sunset means rest, not deliverance.

<u>EXPRESSION</u>

Spin me a tale, boys
web me a rhyme
delight me,
entice me,
unleash your minds.
Dream the spinning acrobat,
tumble hard and get up fast,
don't be last. Last.
Persist forever.
Persist to death.
It is ALL only a test.
Don't choke.
Don't smoke.
Don't rely on your past.
Fast forward is where you're at.
Looking back
living the past
is for pessimists.
don't regret.
Venture = Gains
grow
evolve
bury the plow.
Experience life for it is sacred.
Cherish your life for it is now.
Learn.
Relate.
Be discreet.
You've something to teach.
Edit negative leanings
for expression is the ultimate freedom;
always in fashion,
always in season.

GODSAID

Then God said,
"take this gift,
and this one,
and this one.
I like what you have offered Me.
I like what you have given.
I like the talk you say to Me,
the poem that is your reason.
You please Me."

"Courage follows where truth treads its path to beauty." - TT

PRELUDE TO:
Letters to My Sons *CRY FOR THE NIGHT 1989*

All you can do is watch your children and live your childhood in them. It will never return; and all you can hope is that you can live your life in examples less painfully than your father did; with more joy and freedom from the constraints of the duties we call work.
So when they look out at their children in the yard, they can smile warmly and thank you for the freedom you've allowed them in the work you've done.

REMEMBER: TO ALWAYS BE A GENTLEMAN

Treat everyone you meet with dignity, respect and mutual admiration; from the smallest baby to the oldest lady. It's easy. Be nice. Be polite. Open doors for women, and watch doors open for you toward them. Don't' talk when you're supposed to be listening. Listen. Everything expresses something in some way. Honor that.

Be the person the rest of your friends can depend upon to be a friend. Be true. Cultivate integrity, and you will be treated the same. Raise your voice rarely, it carries more weight that way, it's taken seriously. Anger as a tone turns off and turns away people quickly.

Read, "THE TRUE GENTLEMAN" by John Walter Wayland, and you will understand all you need to succeed at being a gentleman. Take care of your possessions. Keep your clothes and speech neat. Win respect by kissing some ass once in a while but also capitalize on every opportunity to stand up for yourself, fiercely. You can either be a man who's looked up to or who's looked down upon. It's up to you.

You can do all this without being stuffy or self-possessed. Choose to always be a gentleman, appropriate to every occasion, but especially with women. Gentlemen attract gentlewomen. Ask your Mom about that!

REMEMBER: INTEGRITY

It's very tough to teach integrity. Integrity means honoring your work, what you say you'll do, you do.
It's a lot like confidence, and having great integrity helps you gain great confidence, because you start to see yourself accomplishing small things, then larger, then things you can't even imagine, things so big that when you state them, you have no idea how you will possibly pull it off. Integrity knows you'll find a way. By building belief in yourself, making actions follow words, doing things for the benefit of others, doing it with humility, truth, honor, pride and consistency, guarantees that 10 times out of 11 you'll hit your target. 10 times is 100 percent. You hit that, then strive to always get/ give 110%
When you have a reputation for having integrity, you not only get more notice, more work, more rewards, more respect, more license to be liberal with your time and creativity, you also gain notoriety for having integrity.

REMEMBER: YOUR DREAMS

They are something only you can experience. They are entirely of your creation. They filter everything that's happened in your life. There is more color, more depth, more sensation in your dreams than any other spontaneous action in real life. They hold invention. They hold song. They exhilarate. They pave the path to where you're going from where you've been.
In dreams you can visit anyone, in any time and space, and control their, and your, actions, reactions and sentences. You can breathe underwater. You can walk through walls. You're Super, man. You can fly.

You remember your dreams by simply telling yourself, "Tonight, I remember my dreams." With dreams, the more you can remember, the more you can forget, forgive and move past, passively.

Remember the scenes, the scents, the characters, the movement, the vehicles, words, feelings, visions. Remember how you feel when you awaken, any fleeting images, the first thing you see when you open your eyes to daylight. Remember a dominant color. Dreams hold everything. But the most important thing to remember about them is to act on what you've dreamt, because dreams are always something from the past expressed in the present and lost in an instant to the future.

REMEMBER: YOU WILL ALWAYS BE AN ARTIST FIRST
(everything from birth on is formed through your vision)

You design your life, from smallest nuance to cataclysmic event. What you think about, you become. There's no greater artistry than learning to live well, to treat yourself and those around you to all the nicest words, feelings, emotions and memories possible.

In the literal sense, the world is composed of only so many people brave enough to admit they're artists, and then to live that fate. The other end of the spectrum are those who proclaim to be artists and then show no talent nor creativity, or worse yet, ignore the talent and creativity they were given and live only by existing, avoiding the artistry they possess and eternally regretting what they are not giving.

Admit to your artistry, praise it, be thankful for it, and then humbly go about your business of teaching the world what you see through your imagination.

Remember you are an artist first. Invention teaches us how to eat, breathe, feel, live, from infancy on. Words don't tell us how to be or explain what we need, intuition does. What you feel is what you express. Never lose that. An artist must believe in nothing; believe that the emptiness can be something. The artist constantly starts from scratch, then builds, embellishes, decorates. The artist always sees something in nothing as equally as nothing in something.

REMEMBER: TO DESIRE

***You already are and have everything you will ever need in this life.
(but DESIRE all you can.)***

First, let me explain the difference between NEED, WANT and DESIRE.

NEED is something you will never have. It is a possession you can never possess. It's a state of perpetual lack because it's a black hole chasm of emptiness to never be filled. Need is the element you will always have and never have enough of. So as far as you're concerned, it's worthless to pursue anything you NEED. As long as you need, you won't have.

WANT is a passing attraction. It is this car or that stereo, this girl, that friend — a constant ebb and flow of possessions and feelings that you could really live without, but know it would be nice to have around. A want is always temporary. Like need, you will never be without want. As much as you try to fill either of them with meaningless tail-chasing endeavors that take you to an empty box in an abandoned closet, WANT, like NEED, is the ugly stepsister to the DESIRE of Cinderella. WANT is what you needed and no longer care about. To want things is only one step up from the bottom feeders of the food chain of NEED. In life, you always get what you want, then find you really don't want it.

DESIRE is the crown jewel, the only jewel. DESIRE is something you can taste, or feel across your skin, it sends palpitations through your heart, it stirs emotions in the brain and ingenuity in attaining it. Desire is wanting or needing something passionately. It's worth dying for. You'll know desire when you go after something with every thought and action of each day. It pushes you to seek places you'd never imagined, do what you'd never do, be someone so passionately enthralled in the pursuit of that one thing that to others your obsession seems ridiculous, yet to you, it's the pinnacle of your world. Desire is seldom present, but when it arrives, it's exquisitely evident and impossible to ignore. It roars for attention and is not sated until it's accomplished or somehow fulfilled. Its reward is uplifting, often the culmination of time and thought, investment, risk and sometimes outright foolishness. Desire comes, then keeps on coming. It takes prisoners. It coerces and convinces and calls forth forces often reluctant to give in. Desire is the good thing of the want/need/triad.
YOU NEED TO ALWAYS WANT DESIRE. WHEN YOU HAVE IT, YOU HAVE IT ALL.

REMEMBER THIS

The memory is so good it remembers even the things you choose to ignore. It records the first smile your mother gave, the first kiss on a first date, and every nuance of emotion from fear to pure joy. The more you choose to remember of your own volition, the deeper imbedded it becomes. Soak up life. Sponge it up with all the gusto of the first home cooked meal in a month. Eat foods that are so alive they burst and pop with flavor inside your mouth.

Listen in silence to the world offered the ears. Notice sunsets, and full moons, winter brightness, blue skies over blue water seen looking up through 20 feet of the Tidy Bowl sea. Remember friends and all the good things and even the bad. Take to heart a whispered breath on your ear, as it moves over the creases, bringing the lobe's hairs to attention. Remember music and words and books and authors, quote poetry, learn something moving to recite verbatim, remember what you can because the brain will remember the rest. Remember how to take care of your body, honor it with training, diet and recuperation. Remember how good it feels to be alive. Recall how pain feels but don't dwell in it.

Take in every aspect of every thing, the way a newborn sees things for the first time, observant, drinking in, memorizing, studying the lines of a face or the whiskers of a cat, remember that you have an endless supply of storage space in your head and take your life to the end in pursuit of filling it with places and friends, feelings and scenery and beaches and sunsets and embraces and tastes and fragrances from the skin, hair and mouth of that first girlfriend, and the next; check out the petals of flowers and the symmetry, balance and beauty that God creates with. Remember manners and dreams and directions and birthdays. Remember artists and teachers and idols and leaders and the stranger who lent you a hand.

In a day an array of seemingly mundane events occur, yet somewhere hidden in the homework or TV show or demand from parents is a hidden germ of what you must learn. Like each raindrop carries a grain of dirt, each insignificant quirk has something in it to learn from, so remember. Remember all that moves you, to tears, to joy, to sorrow, to euphoria. Your heart and brain were meant to feel those things; memory is the chain that links the life in little vignettes from birth to death. So remember everything in between as only you were meant to experience it. And then if you still so choose to forget, just remember this,

I Love You,   Dad

<u>THE CREED</u>

This circle is a barrier which
protects our family.
No harm can come to us,
no danger can penetrate our love.
Nothing is closer nor stronger than our family.

This circle symbolizes unending love
for all people and for all things.
We move and act in a spirit of peace
with kind words spoken,
arguments avoided,
and positive attitudes displayed

We honor each other with kindness
with encouragement and with support
We mutually admire and respect each other as individuals,
each capable of all we dream we can be,
with possibilities and opportunities more numerous than we
can count.

We are fortunate.
We are blessed. We are grateful for all we have to learn and
to teach.

We are thankful that God has chosen us to share our time as
a family;
that He cares so much about us and trusts us so much,
to give us the responsibilities of all
our gifts and talents and knowledge.

We are thankful for the love and joy God gives us in such
abundance.
We are thankful to have all we desire, enough to share with
others
and recirculate to those less fortunate.

We care for Gods earth,
for His plants, animals and water,
for the beautiful mountain's and skies,
for our food, our shelter, our clothes,
our tools, machines and instruments of work and relaxation.

We honor God with all we create
from the smallest sentence, to the largest sculpture
in song, in dance, in actions;
because God moves through us in our creativity.

God is our strength, our love, our life.
And we thank Him.

With this circle we begin a new level of being.
If we are scared,
if a situation makes one of us feel weak,
think of this circle and realize your strength is 5 times greater.

If temptations or questions arise
and you are unsure which path is right,
this circle brings you back to peace
by knowing everything leads back to us, to our love,
and it will always be here.

If something weighs heavy on your mind
and there is no right or wrong answer,
let your mind be freed into this ring of understanding where our
experiences together can dissolve any uneasiness
where you can find comfort in believing
we all share a burden as equally as we share freedom.

There is nothing, together, we can't defeat.
When loneliness or alienation come creeping in,
when you feel all alone,
when you feel you're not living
remember this circle of friendship,
think of our laughter, our smiles, our tears.
Because we shared these too.
They make us stronger,
they are what makes us unique in this world of strangers.
This family. These memories. These years.

Think of this circle without beginning or end,
a private sun emanating growth, warmth, friendship and strength;
a barrier protecting our beliefs, our dreams, our ambitions.
We are the epitome of what family means.
Believe that, unconditionally, and we'll have everything we need
in the world within these boundaries.

Believe the Creed
Our Circle means our family
A Ring into Infinity-
A Concentric Wave Everreaching.

Believe in goodness.
Believe in health.
Believe in strength.
Believe in wealth.
Believe in Love.
Believe in everything there is to believe in,
because You are endless creativity.

You fill our dreams, our lives, our desires.
You, God, see and know everything.
We only have to believe,
You fill in the details.

You give us colors and sense to experience them;
You give us sounds and let us vibrate with them.
You give us personalities with incongruities and eccentricities.
You made us unique as snowflakes.
Yo give us will and possibility.
We believe, and give thanks.

Spencer Blake Typinski
Zachary Neil Typinski
Thomas John Typinski II
Deborah Kay Typinski
Tom Typinski - Easter 1985